BUSINESS FINANCE 101

BY E. DEAN BROWN, JR.

ISBN: 1-4196-5578-7
ISBN-13: 9781419655784
Library of Congress Control Number: 2008905150

Visit www.booksurge.com to order additional copies.

Acknowledgments

To my wife, Monica, thank you so much for all of the encouragement, wisdom, and caring. I am here, because you were there.

To my kids, Tre, Jessica, Larc, and Lachance, thanks for inspiring me to try to be a better father and provider. If you think about it, I wouldn't be a father without you!

To my parents, thanks for staying on my case when it came to God, school, relationships, and life.

To all the students I have taught, thank you. It has been a blast!

My name is E. Dean Brown, Jr. For the past ten years or so, I've been the controller for a variety of companies in different industries. I am a CPA and an MBA. In addition, I am an adjunct professor at a private university.

Why Did I Write This Book?

In my career, I've worked for individuals who don't understand the basics of financial statements, how to read them, or what they represent. I have had a hard time trying to explain it to them; some of them just don't get it.

Some people I've worked for were wise enough to know their financial statement knowledge limitations and were humble enough to admit it. I think that is great! It allowed me to work with them, to teach them. It is harder with the ones who think they know, and really don't know, or know they don't know and want you to believe they do know. That's like me telling a patient I know how to perform brain surgery, as I Google "Brain Surgery Procedures".

Trust me; accountants get very frustrated working with people who are in financial statement knowledge denial. I had an experience one time when I started working for a new company. The company had been in business for over ten years. The owner was creating the financial statements before giving them to the tax accountant for annual review and income tax calculation. So I created the financial statements for the current month and presented them to the owner. The owner asked what the brackets were around the number at the bottom. I explained to him that the figure represented a net loss for the month. The owner said that was impossible; there was money in the bank. I am not kidding, that conversation actually took place.

So one day I was having lunch with my longtime friend Jeff Foster. He mentioned that there was a private university that was looking for someone to teach advanced auditing. I was an auditor a number of years ago, before I became a controller. I was reluctant at first. I didn't think I could teach.

I e-mailed the director of education at the school. We spoke and arranged for me to come in and give a small presentation example of me teaching a class. He said I could give it on anything I wanted to. So I chose investing.

I am a part-time investor and I really enjoy it. I enjoy reading the *Financial Times, Business Week, Fortune,* and *Forbes* magazines, looking at stocks and options, etc. So, I decided to teach on buying stocks and options and on trading strategies. They told me it should last about ten minutes. I began my presentation, and twenty minutes later they told me to stop. They asked me to step outside and wait while they decided what to do with me. I could hear them. They weren't talking about me; they were talking about what I said in the presentation. The director of education walked out and told me I had the job. That was the beginning of a great ride!

So, I started teaching. The first class I taught was advanced auditing. The next class was accounting forensics. Then, I taught applied managerial finance. I had a blast teaching that class. Now, I must tell you that about 50% to 60% of my classes are filled with international students. I have students from Ghana, Libya, Mongolia, China, Ethiopia, Liberia, Sri Lanka, India, Singapore, Palestine, Morocco, etc. No, I can't speak any of these languages; however teaching the international students is the biggest challenge and the most fun. I know, because of language limitations, they don't understand about 10% of what I say. Some of the international students have told me that. But I keep saying the same thing in different ways. Then all of a sudden I see their eyes light up and I know **they got it**! That's a blast!

So, I concluded that if I can teach international students finance and I can teach my bosses finance, why not do something for everyone else? That's why I wrote this book.

Why Should You Understand Financial Statements?

Should every business owner or department/regional manager of a company understand financial statements? **YES!** How can you effectively understand your business, the impact of your revenue, the impact of your costs, your cost structure, expenses, profit, etc.? How can you put together a budget or fill out a loan application without understanding financial statements? How can you answer the loan officer's questions if you don't understand the reason for the questions? How do you even know if you are making money?

So here you are, in a new position or you were just promoted to one, and you want to have a turbocharged introduction to finance. The purpose of this book is to give a high-level view of how finance works for people who don't have the time to take accounting or finance courses but feel they need to learn more about this subject as fast as possible.

So, get in, buckle up and hold on. Let's go for a ride, have some fun, and learn about finance.

Financial Statements?

Let's start out with, **"What are financial statements?"**

Financial statements are the report cards for companies' financial performance over a certain period of time. Remember when you were a kid in school? At the end of each semester and sometimes in between you received either a report card or a progress report that you had to take home to your parents. I don't know about you, but those were some very traumatic times for me. That was some serious stress on an eight-year-old kid. I played around in school too much and my report card showed it. The last thing I wanted to do was have to answer for what my parents were about to see, because there were consequences to pay! However, I thank God they stayed on my case when it came to my grades. It wasn't easy for them, but they kept the faith.

Anyway, a corporate financial statement is also a report card or progress report. Sometimes, when executives give their financial report card to their stockholders, lenders, and Wall Street analysts and the report is not that good, they feel the same way

I did at eight years old, when I had to answer to my parents. I guess the advantage I had was I knew my parents weren't going to fire me. I'm sure they thought about it though! Yeah, but at eight years old I was too cute to be fired.

So, what is this financial report card comprised of? The financial statements are comprised of three different compilations of accounting information: the **Balance Sheet**, the **Income Statement,** and the **Statement of Cash Flows**. These have a significant amount of the information needed to make a decision. In some situations, this is all the information you have to make a decision, unless you have direct access to management.

So let's look at the individual sections of the financial statements.

BALANCE SHEET

Let's start with the Balance Sheet. Accounting personnel construct the financial statements. Now, accounting is very time sensitive. By that I mean that accounting information is useful for only the time period that it is reporting; not only that, it is reporting what was in the past.

If you take a look at Generally Accepted Accounting Principles (GAAP) there are a lot of rules that dictate when things are supposed to be "recognized" or reported, especially expenses and revenue. You can't report either too soon or too late, in relation to when the transaction took place. If you do, they commonly refer to that as "cooking" the books. Cooking the books can get you a new address in a jail cell.

There are many, many examples of people who have tried doing that and gotten caught. Let me tell you, it's not worth it. I heard a man say one time, "Do what's right, do it because it's right, then do it right." That is a great saying and well worth remembering. Also, it doesn't sit well with investors when the information comes out about what happened with the financial statements. There are big and small investors relying on information that is "current, accurate, and complete" to make decisions with either large or small amounts of money. They want accurate information. Warren Buffet once said, "It is easier to stay out of trouble then to get out of trouble."

Back to the Balance Sheet, the Balance Sheet covers the time period "as of" a certain date.

For example, below is the Balance Sheet for Coca-Cola is dated as of December 31, 2007. Do you see that? So, all the asset and liability categories have a value as of December 31, 2007.

The Balance Sheet consists of assets, liabilities, and stockholders' equity. The assets are things that have a value placed on them. This includes, but is not limited to cash, accounts receivable, marketable securities, investments, inventory, fixed assets, and the like. An asset account increases in value when the company purchases something or decreases in value when it sells something, except for cash.

Assets are listed by liquidity hierarchy. The more liquid an asset, the higher up on the Balance Sheet it is. The definition of liquid or liquidity is basically, how fast (in units of time) you can turn the asset into cash.

Take a look at Coca-Cola's Balance Sheet below and you will see what I mean.

Coca-Cola Co. (KO)

Source: www.yahoo.com/finance

Balance Sheet

All numbers in thousands

PERIOD ENDING	31-Dec-07
Cash And Cash Equivalents	4,093,000
Short Term Investments	215,000
Net Receivables	3,317,000
Inventory	2,220,000
Other Current Assets	2,260,000
Total Current Assets	**12,105,000**
Long Term Investments	7,777,000
Property Plant and Equipment	8,493,000
Goodwill	4,256,000
Intangible Assets	7,963,000
Accumulated Amortization	-
Other Assets	2,675,000
Deferred Long Term Asset Charges	-
Total Assets	**43,269,000**
Accounts Payable	7,173,000
Short/Current Long Term Debt	6,052,000
Other Current Liabilities	-
Total Current Liabilities	**13,225,000**
Long Term Debt	3,277,000
Other Liabilities	3,133,000
Deferred Long Term Liability Charges	1,890,000

Minority Interest	-
Negative Goodwill	-
Total Liabilities	**21,525,000**
Misc Stocks Options Warrants	-
Redeemable Preferred Stock	-
Preferred Stock	-
Common Stock	880,000
Retained Earnings	36,235,000
Treasury Stock	(23,375,000)
Capital Surplus	7,378,000
Other Stockholder Equity	626,000
Total Stockholder Equity	**21,744,000**

ASSETS

The first category under ASSETS is **Current Assets**. Current Assets are assets that are expected to be converted to cash within one accounting cycle, usually twelve months. The first category under Current Assets is **Cash and Cash Equivalents**. We see Coca-Cola has $4,093,000 in cash and cash equivalents. Now, you are probably asking yourself, why Coca-Cola has only $4,093,000 in cash. A multibillion dollar international company has only $4,093,000 in cash and cash equivalents? Well, it's not $4,093,000, but $4,093,000,000. If you look at the top of the column you will see "all numbers in thousands." So, in order to see the real number, just take the number and multiply it by one thousand

and you will get the real value. From here on, I'll be referring to the number issued in the financial statements.

The next line item is **Short Term Investment**. Short term investments are very liquid securities that can be converted to cash quickly at a reasonable price. In any case, their maturities are usually a year or less. Certificates of deposit, commercial paper, treasury bills, and the like are examples. If an organization owns any of these items, it can sell them on the open market at a reasonable price.

The next item is **Net Receivables**. Net receivables are made up of two different components. Accounts receivable minus bad debts. Accounts receivables are funds you expect to receive from another company that has purchased your goods or services. In Coke's case, they would expect to receive funds from bottlers that have purchased their cola syrup. Bad debts are accounts receivable or an estimation of accounts receivable that you have determined you won't be able to collect.

Now the reason this item is a little lower on the list is because, usually the company that bought the goods that created the receivables doesn't have to pay for it for a certain time frame. In a lot of cases, when a sale is made, the buyer has thirty days to remit to, or pay, the seller. Now, this depends on agreements the sellers and buyers have. You will also find terminology like 2% 10 Net /30 or similar to that. What this means is that if the buyer exercises the option to pay the invoice by the tenth day after the invoice date, the buyer can reduce the amount by 2%. If the option is not exercised, then the full amount is due within thirty days. This provides incentive for buyers to pay quickly.

Why would the seller offer such a discount to pay early? It provides a better cash flow for the company. Companies are run by cash flow. Why would the buyer want to take the cash discount? It reduces the buyer's costs. However, sometimes it isn't worth it. I've seen cash discounts amount to a total of $1.65. You have to ask yourself if it is worth paying an invoice early, to receive a $1.65 discount. You have to assess your situation and determine if it is worth it.

Inventories are next. This is amount of product that is sitting in warehouses or in various stages of production that has not been sold yet. This amount on Coke's statements is $2,220,000. For manufacturing and production companies, this is usually a large number. Inventories require a lot of cash. As the saying goes, you have to spend it to make it. Well, you have to spend money in the form of direct material, direct labor, etc. to produce the product before it can be sold in its finished form. With Coke, you are going to have raw materials like sugar, water, and everything else in the secret recipe.

Other Current Assets are exactly that. This is a collection of assets that really don't have their own category for reasons left up to the company.

That's it for Current Assets. At the bottom of the column you will see the total amount for Current Assets of $12,105,000.

Some companies have a category called Prepaid Assets. Believe it or not, you can prepay expenses. You can prepay your electric bill before it's due, can't you? This is not really the same thing, but let me give you an example. As I said earlier, accounting is time sensitive. According to GAAP, accrual accounting says that you record the activity in the period that it was transacted. Near the end of the fiscal year, an organization may have paid some insurance expenses that are for the next fiscal year, but paid in the current fiscal year. Since you have to record the transaction when it happened, it would be recorded as a prepaid expense. However, in the new fiscal year, it will be journalized or moved from prepaid expenses to the related insurance expense account.

The next section is a collection of Long Term Investments, Fixed Assets, Goodwill Intangible Assets, etc.

LONG TERM INVESTMENTS

If the company you are analyzing has significant investments in other companies that would force it to report the investment using the equity method, this is where it would be reported.

I'm not going into much detail here regarding the equity method. That is for a more advanced accounting level, and all we are trying to do with this book is give you the basics. However, companies that own 20%–49% of another company report the ownership using the equity method. The equity method represents the ownership of the other company versus the legal ownership. Therefore, the company reports the owned portion of the other company as net income or loss. For example, if Company A owns 30% of Company B, and Company B's net income is $1,000,000, and then Company A would show 30% ($300,000) of that net income on the Income Statement. Now, if Company A owns 50% or more of Company B, the assumption is that Company A can wield significant influence and

Company A must consolidate financial statements with Company B.

PROPERTY PLANT & EQUIPMENT OR FIXED ASSETS

Fixed assets are assets that are usually high-dollar costs, have a long life, and are not easily or quickly sold. Examples of fixed assets are property, buildings, autos, furniture, equipment, etc. Now the difference with fixed assets is that their book value are adjusted or reduced for deprecation or amortization.

Depreciation is an expense that is designed to recognize or reduce the economic value of the asset over a certain time period. Now, understand that the market value of the asset may be actually increasing in value, but the expense is calculated and deducted from the cost. Here is an example: Your company constructed a building for $1,000,000. We are going to depreciate the building over thirty years. GAAP allows you to accelerate the depreciation of the building for tax purposes, but for our purpose we'll assume straight line depreciation. What is straight line? Take the $1,000,000 divide it by thirty years and you will have $33,333 per year of depreciation. On the Income Statement that would show up under "Depreciation Expense" and is a deduction in expenses that is included in the calculation of net income.

Depreciation is applied to fixed assets, assets that you can touch. Now there are assets that are amortized over certain periods of time. Theses assets are Goodwill, Patents, Leases, Trademarks, etc. A little different asset, you can't go up and touch one of these. Well, I guess in some cases you can; patents are paperwork.

Now we are done with talking about assets. Depending on the company, industry, country, etc., you could have more or fewer accounts. What I have described are the basics.

So, the value of the assets as of December 31, 2007, was $43,269,000.

OK, we have explained the assets side. Now, let's take a look at the liabilities and stockholders' equity.

LIABILITIES

Current Liabilities

Liabilities are obligations. Like assets, there is a hierarchy here also. The liabilities that are due the earliest will be higher up on the list. Current liabilities are liabilities that are expected to be paid within a year.

Let's go back to our example of Coca-Cola. Look at the first line item. Accounts Payable. Accounts payable are those liabilities that you owe to your vendors, material suppliers, subcontractors, etc. These are the companies they bought the sugar from, the water, etc. If you think about it, an accounts payable to Coca-Cola is an accounts receivable to the company that Coca-Cola bought the product from.

When the invoice comes in, accounting will record it to the appropriate expense account and the other side of the entry will go to the Accounts Payable account. This is like a holding tank. It has the date the invoice was entered, when it's due to be paid, related discounts, etc. Then when it is time to pay the vendors, the accounting person can open up Accounts Payable and it will show who should be paid next and so on. You might be wondering why payroll doesn't show up under Current Liabilities. Payroll is for employees and employees aren't vendors. Also, there are more cost line items associated with payroll. For example, various taxing authorities want their money, 401K deposits, etc.

Let's take a sidetrack. The financial statements that are shown don't show a line item for Accrued

Expenses. In most companies there are Accrued Expenses. However, in the consolidation of these financial statements, they have rolled them up into another line item. Anyway, Accrued Expenses are expenses that you know are there, and you have paid them, but they need to be moved to a different account in a future period, for example, Accrued Labor. It's like Prepaid Expenses, but on the liability side. Let's say that labor closes or cuts off on the twenty-seventh of the month. There are still three more workdays, but they go on the "next" check. However, they are the current month's expense. So what you do is calculate the labor for those three days. You record it as labor expense and the other side is Accrued Labor. Now, when the next month comes a long, you are going to "reverse" that transaction. So, on the first of the next month you reverse the transaction and record it. Why? Because those three days will be recorded when the paychecks are run, but in the new month.

The next item is **Short/Current Long Term Debt**. This the current portion of the long term debt. In other words, investors, bankers, etc. want to see how much is owed, but they also want to see what is owed in the current period. Look at it this way; let's assume you have a thirty year mortgage. Your current portion of the mortgage would be what you would pay this year.

The last item is Other Current Liabilities. Like other assets, this category is a collection of liabilities that don't have a separate category.

The total amount of Total Current Liabilities as of December 31, 2007, is $13,225,000.

Now we are going to finish off the rest of the liabilities.

Long Term Liabilities are the liabilities that mature in more than a year. These include long term notes, mortgages, etc.

Other Liabilities are just like the Other Assets and other Current Liabilities. No further explanation required.

Deferred Long Term Liability charges are charges that are being deferred.

Minority Interest reflects the claim on assets belonging to other, non-controlling shareholders.

Negative Goodwill is when a company buys another company at a price that less than the value of the assets.

As you can see, Coke doesn't have any Minority Interest or Negative Goodwill.

STOCKHOLDERS' EQUITY

The last item is **Stockholders' Equity**. Stockholders' Equity is interesting. The number of line items reported in it depends largely on the company and its industry.

Taking a look at Coke's we see that there is Redeemable Stock, Preferred Stock, Common Stock, Additional Paid-In Capital, and, probably one of the most important line items, Retained Earnings.

Preferred Stock is sometimes referred to as a hybrid stock. It has features of a loan and of a stock. The primary feature of Preferred Stock is the dividend payments. Preferred Stock has a feature called cumulative dividends. If the company decides not to pay dividends, for whatever reason, the Preferred Stock's dividends accumulate such that, when the company decides to pay dividends, the Preferred Dividends will get paid prior to Common Stock dividends.

The second feature is that upon the company's liquidation, preferred stock will get paid before Common Stock. In addition, some preferred shares have special voting rights, for the purpose of voting on special events. However, for the most part, Preferred Stock doesn't have any voting shares. But, if the preferred shares are greatly in arrears for a substantial amount of time, they can gain voting rights. In other words, they can take on the shape of some of Common Stock characteristics.

There isn't any Preferred Stock recorded in Coke's financials.

Common Stock is more commonly known and traded in the financial markets. It rises and falls on news, speculation, and real-life occurrences on the stock market. What I mean by real-life occurrences is that an economic or global event can affect the stock market. A refinery that gets damaged in a hurricane can drive up oil prices. However, the hurricane affected only one refinery. One company in an industry can report negative earnings and sometimes that one report can drive down the other stocks in the same industry. However, the other companies may not report their earnings for a few more months.

Retained Earnings shows the "to date value" of all of the income and losses since the company was created.

Treasury Stock is the stock that was bought back by the company. In the case of Coca-Cola, they bought back $23,375,000 of stock. It is subtracted from stockholders' equity.

Capital Surplus is the amount of cash received over the par value of the stock.

Other Stockholder Equity could be a number of things. They are important enough to be placed in the Stockholders' Equity section, however, not important enough to have a separate category. If you are interested in what these items are, usually they can be found in the 10-K or 10-Q financial reports filed with the Securities Exchange Commission (SEC). The Web site for the SEC is www.sec.gov.

So the total amount of Stockholder Equity as of December 31, 2007, is $21,744,000.

INCOME STATEMENT

The Income Statement is probably the most known and recognized of the financial statements, specifically for two pieces of data: sales and net income, also called the **Bottom Line**. However, there are many parts to it, starting with sales and ending with net income. Each of these line items tells a piece of the company's story.

Coca-Cola Co. (KO)
Source: www.yahoo.com/finance
Income Statement

All numbers in thousands

PERIOD ENDING	31-Dec-07
Total Revenue	**28,857,000**
Cost of Revenue	10,406,000
Gross Profit	**18,451,000**
Research Development	-
Selling General and Administrative	11,199,000
Non Recurring	-
Others	-
Total Operating Expenses	-
Operating Income or Loss	**7,252,000**
Total Other Income/Expenses Net	1,077,000
Earnings Before Interest And Taxes	8,329,000
Interest Expense	456,000
Income Before Tax	7,873,000
Income Tax Expense	1,892,000
Minority Interest	-
Net Income From Continuing Ops	5,981,000
Discontinued Operations	-
Extraordinary Items	-
Effect Of Accounting Changes	-

Other Items   -
Net Income   **5,981,000**
Preferred Stock And Other Adjustments   -
Net Income Applicable   **$5,981,000**
To Common Shares

The first line we see in Coke's Income Statement is **Sales** of $28,857,000, remember that's billion dollars. Of course, whatever company it is, this figure represents everything your organization sells, whether it is goods, services, or anything like that.

The next line is **Cost of Revenue** or in many cases **Cost of Goods Sold**. Now, this line item represents the direct costs used in the production of the product or service that was sold. What goes into Cost of Goods Sold? These would include, but are not limited to, direct labor, direct material, subcontracting, overhead allocation, etc. A lot of it depends on the business and industry.

Direct Labor is different from administrative labor. Direct Labor is associated with the cost of actually producing the product or service, the "hands on" costs. If you are a construction company, direct labor would include your carpenters, laborers, etc. If you are a manufacturing company, this could include your laser cutters, assemblers, etc. If you are lawn care service, this would include your employees who cut, trim, and edge the lawn. See the difference?

Also included in Cost of Goods Sold are **Materials**. Again, this would include material going into the product. If you are a construction company, this might include lumber, nails, concrete, etc. If you are manufacturing company, this could include sheet metal, wiring, nuts and bolts, etc.

If you subtract Cost of Goods Sold from Sales you get **Gross** profit. Don't get gross profit confused with net profit, which we will discuss later. Gross profit is how much profit you made, during a particular time period, from the goods you sold. It is desirable to have this number as large as possible. Why? Because gross profit is used to pay for all of the support costs in creating the product as well. Administrative support costs can eat into gross profits pretty quickly. Ideally, you want gross profit and net profit to be positive numbers.

Now, we go into Administrative Costs. These are support costs for the creation of the product. These costs include, but are not limited to, depreciation, amortization, bank charges, administrative salaries, rent, telephone charges, advertising, dues and subscriptions, employee benefits, insurance, building maintenance, legal and accounting, travel, etc. See why the gross profit has to be high? Usually there are a lot of administrative costs and they are paid for with the gross profits.

Now, if you deduct administrative costs from gross profit, you have **net profit or net income**. This is the bottom line, how much you made after all expenses have been paid for. Hopefully, this number is a positive number. If not, you might have to review your expenses to see where you can make some reductions over the next period.

Remember, that net income is what is used to calculate your income taxes. So, it is very likely that you can have a line item that says…Earnings Before Taxes (EBT), then a line that is called Taxes, then a line after that called Earnings After Taxes (EAT).

CASH FLOW STATEMENT

This statement has specific uses for certain people. The small-time investor or business owner usually doesn't use it or in some cases doesn't know what it is. So, let's touch on it here. The Cash Flow Statement is what its title says; it traces the cash flow.

Coca-Cola Co. (KO)

Source: www.yahoo.com/finance
Cash Flow

All numbers in thousands

PERIOD ENDING	31-Dec-07
Net Income	**5,981,000**
Depreciation	1,163,000
Adjustments To Net Income	-
Changes In Accounts Receivables	(406,000)
Changes In Liabilities	914,000
Changes In Inventories	(258,000)
Changes In Other Operating Activities	244,000)
Total Cash Flow From Operating Activities	**7,150,000**
Capital Expenditures	(1,648,000)
Investments	349,000
Other Cash Flows from Investing Activities	(5,420,000)
Total Cash Flows From Investing Activities	**(6,719,000)**
Dividends Paid	(3,149,000)
Sale Purchase of Stock	(219,000)
Net Borrowings	4,341,000

Other Cash Flows from Financing Activities	-
Total Cash Flows From Financing Activities	**973,000**
Effect Of Exchange Rate Changes	249,000
Change In Cash and Cash Equivalents	**$1,653,000**

We will start with **Cash from Operating Activities**. This statement starts with Net Income, adds back Deprecation and then on down the line. Why does it add back Depreciation? We add Depreciation and Amortization back to Net Income because, even though they are expenses, they are *non-cash* items, or they don't affect cash in any way. If you remember from earlier in this book, Depreciation represents the reduction of value in a specific asset. But, this recognition of expense is performed with a journal entry. For example,

	Debit	Credit
Depreciation Expense	$5,000	
Accumulated Depreciation		$5,000

See? No cash accounts.

Since cash was not used, it's a non-cash expense, but it is deducted as an expense to achieve Net Income. So you have to add it back to Net Income. It is the same thing with Amortization.

The next category we will look at it is **Cash from Investment Activities**. The title speaks for itself, but what are investment activities? Primarily, these are investments and sales in large assets, such as machinery, plant and equipment, etc.

The next category is **Cash from Financing Activities.** Again, the title speaks for itself. These costs and increases include loans, cash dividends issuing, retiring of debt, etc.

FINANCIAL ANALYSIS

Now that we have covered the basics of financial statements, let's take a look at how to use the information. In and of itself, what does it say? For example, for the period ending December 31, 2007, Coke showed a net income of $5,981,000. So? Is that good or bad? We don't know unless we can compare it to something, maybe to last year or to another company. First, let's look at some financial statement ratios.

There are some key ratios that many organizations use for specific purposes. Mostly, these ratios are used for the purpose of evaluation, to determine if an investment will be made or if a loan shall be given. Because they are ratios, it is easier to compare with other companies or time periods.

The basic ratios and their categories are as follows:

Liquidity Ratios:
- Current Ratio: Current Assets/Current Liabilities
- Quick Ratio: (Current Assets – Inventory)/Current Liabilities
- Cash Ratio: (Cash + Marketable Securities)/Current Liabilities

Activity Ratios:
- Average Collection Period: Accounts Receivable/Average Daily Sales
- Average Payment Period: Average Accounts Receivable/(Sales/Period of Accounting Statements)
- Inventory Turnover Ratio: 1) Sales/Inventory OR 2) Cost of Goods Sold/Average Inventory

Debt Ratios:
- Debt Ratio or Debt to Assets Ratio: Total Liabilities/Total Assets
- Debt to Equity Ratio: Total Liabilities/Stockholders' Equity
- Interest Coverage Ratio or Times Interest Earned Ratio: Earnings Before Interest and Taxes (EBIT)/Interest Coverage
- Long Term Debt to Total Assets Ratio: Long Term Debt/Total Assets

- Debt Service Coverage Ratio: Net Operating Income/Total Debt Service

Profitability Ratios:
- Gross Income Margin: Gross Profit/Sales
- Net Income Margin: Net Income/Sales
- Return on Assets: Net Income/Total Assets
- Return on Equity: Net Income/Average Stockholders' Equity

Market Ratios
- Payout Ratio: 1) Dividends/Net Income, 2) Yearly Dividend per Share/ Earnings per Share
- P/E Ratio: Stock Price per Share/Earnings per Share
- Cash Flow Ratio: Cash Flow from Operations/ Current Liabilities
- Price Book Value Ratio: Stock Price/(Total Assets – Intangible Assets and Liabilities)
- Price/Sales Ratio: Share Price/Revenue per Share
- PEG Ratio: (Stock Price/Annual Earnings)/% of Annual Growth

Dividend Policy Ratios:
- Dividend Yield – Annual Dividends per Share/Price per Share

Now, I'm sure you are wondering what these ratios mean. So, we'll go through most of them and do a little comparison between Coca-Cola Company and Pepsi. I have included Pepsi's financials at the end of the book. Based on that information, let's continue.

Current Ratio: Current Assets/Current Liabilities

Coca-Cola Current Assets	$12,105
Coca-Cola Current Liabilities	$13,225
Coca-Cola Current Ratio	**91.5%**

Pepsi Current Assets	$10,151
Pepsi Current Liabilities	$7,753
Pepsi Current Ratio	**130.9%**

As you can see, Pepsi's current ratio is much better than Coca-Cola's. Does that mean Pepsi is a better company? Not necessarily, it just means that Coca-Cola and Pepsi manage their companies differently. They have different goals, objections, targets, etc. and, as a result, manage their current assets and liabilities differently.

Quick Ratio: (Current Assets - Inventory)/Current Liabilities

Coca-Cola Current Assets – Inventory	$9,885
Coca-Cola Liabilities	$13,225
Coca-Cola Quick Ratio	**74.7%**

Pepsi Current Assets – Inventory	$7,861
Pepsi Current Liabilities	$7,753
Pepsi Quick Ratio	**101.4%**

Cash Ratio: (Cash + Marketable Securities)/Current Liabilities

Coca-Cola Cash + Marketable Securities	$4,308
Coca-Cola Liabilities	$13,225
Coca-Cola Cash Ratio	**32.6%**

Pepsi Cash + Marketable Securities	$2,481
Pepsi Current Liabilities	$7,753
Pepsi Cash Ratio	**32.0%**

Average Collection Period: Accounts Receivable/ Average Daily Sales

Coca-Cola Accounts Receivable - Net	$3,317
Coca-Cola Average Daily Sales	
(Sales($28,857)/365 days)	$79
Coca-Cola Average Collection Days	41.96

Pepsi Accounts Receivable - Net	$4,389
Pepsi Average Daily Sales	
(Sales ($39,474)/365 days)	$108
Pepsi Average Collect Days	40.59

(Note: I am assuming all sales are on credit.)

Inventory Turnover Ratio: Sales/Inventory (One Calculation)

Coca-Cola Sales	$28,857
Coca-Cola Inventory	$2,220
Coca-Cola Inventory Turnover	13.00
Pepsi Sales	$39,474
Pepsi Inventory	$2,290
Pepsi Inventory Turnover	**17.24**

Inventory Turnover Ratio: Sales/Inventory (Another Calculation)

Coca-Cola Cost of Goods Sold	$10,406
Coca-Cola Inventory	$2,220
Coca-Cola Inventory Turnover	**4.69**

Inventory Turnover Ratio: Sales/Inventory (Another Calculation)

Pepsi Cost of Goods Sold	$18,038
Pepsi Inventory	$2,290
Pepsi Inventory Turnover	**7.88**

Debt Ratio Or Debt to Assets Ratio: Total Debt/Total Assets

Coca-Cola Total Liabilities	$21,525
Coca-Cola Total Assets	$43,269
Coca-Cola Debt Ratio	**49.7%**

Pepsi Total Liabilities	$17,394
Pepsi Total Assets	$34,628
Pepsi Debt Ratio	**50.2%**

Long Term Debt to Total Assets Ratio: Long Term Debt/Total Assets

Coca-Cola Long Debt	$3,277
Coca-Cola Total Assets	$43,269
Coca-Cola Debt Ratio	**7.6%**

Pepsi Long Debt	$4,203
Pepsi Total Assets	$34,628
Pepsi Debt Ratio	**12.1%**

Debt to Equity Ratio: Total Debt/Total Equity

Coca-Cola Total Liabilities	$21,525
Coca-Cola Total Equity	$21,744
Coca-Cola Debt Ratio	**99%**

Pepsi Total Liabilities	$17,394
Pepsi Total Equity	$17,234
Pepsi Debt Ratio	**100.9%**

Interest Coverage Ratio or Times Interest Earned Ratio: EBIT/Interest Coverage

Coca-Cola Earnings Before Interest Taxes	$8,329
Coca-Cola Interest	$456
Coca-Cola Times Interest Earned	**18.27**

Pepsi Earnings Before Interest Taxes	$7,855
Pepsi Interest	$224
Pepsi Times Interest Earned	**35.07**

Gross Profit Margin: Gross Profit/Sales

Coca-Cola Gross Profit	$18,451
Coca-Cola Sales	$28,857
Coca-Cola Gross Profit Margin	**63.9%**

Pepsi Gross Profit	$21,436
Pepsi Sales	$39,474
Pepsi Gross Profit Margin	**54.3%**

Net Profit Margin: Net Profit/Sales

Coca-Cola Net Profit	$5,981
Coca-Cola Sales	$28,857
Coca-Cola Net Profit Margin	**20.7%**

Pepsi Net Profit	$5,658
Pepsi Sales	$39,474
Pepsi Net Profit Margin	**14.3%**

Return on Assets: Net Income/Total Assets

Coca-Cola Net Profit	$5,981
Coca-Cola Total Assets	$43,269
Coca-Cola Return on Assets	**13.8%**

Pepsi Net Profit	$5,658
Pepsi Total Assets	$34,628
Pepsi Return on Assets	**16.3%**

Return on Equity: Net Income / Average Stockholders' Equity

Coca-Cola Net Profit	$5,981
Coca-Cola Total Stockholders' Equity	$21,744
Coca-Cola Return on Equity	**27.5%**

Pepsi Net Profit	$5,658
Pepsi Total Stockholders' Equity	$17,234
Pepsi Return on Equity	**32.8%**

There are many more ratios you can use to assist you in evaluating a company. I just touched on what I consider the most important.

OK, what does all of this mean? A ratio doesn't mean anything unless it can be compared to something. Check this out. If I told you XYZ Company experienced a 21% profit margin fiscal year-end 2007, what would you say? Nothing, unless you can compare it to, for example, the previous year or another company in the same industry.

That brings me to Coca-Cola and Pepsi. Let's take a look.

Based on the information above, we can compare the companies.

The reason I chose Coca-Cola and Pepsi is because the world knows these companies and they are pretty similar. The exception is that Pepsi has diversified into snacks, but for our purposes it is close enough.

OK, the ratios are as follows:

Profitability Ratios

Profit Margin
Coca-Cola	Pepsi
20.7%	14.3%

Return on Assets
Coca-Cola	Pepsi
13.8%	16.3%

Return on Equity
Coca-Cola	Pepsi
27.5%	32.8%

Asset Utilization Ratios
Average Collection Period (Days)
Coca-Cola	Pepsi
41.96	40.59

Inventory Turnover Ratio (First Calc.)

Coca-Cola   Pepsi

13.00   17.24

Inventory Turnover Ratio (Second Calc.)

Coca-Cola   Pepsi

4.69   7.88

Liquidity Ratios
Current Ratio

Coca-Cola   Pepsi

91.5%   130.9%

Quick Ratio

Coca-Cola   Pepsi

74.7%   101.4%

Debt Utilization Ratios
Total Debt to Total Assets

Coca-Cola   Pepsi

49.7%   50.2%

Times Interest Earned

Coca-Cola   Pepsi

18.27   35.07

Profit ratios for Coke and Pepsi differ by 6.4%. For multiple-billion-dollar companies, 6.4% is a lot, and in dollars or euros it can be quite a bit also.

Now, let's take a look at the other categories, but we'll put "win" in the columns under the company that won.

Coca-Cola

Net Profit Margin	Win
Debt Ratio	Win
Long Term Debt/Ratio	Win

<u>Pepsi</u>

Current Ratio	Win
Quick Ratio	Win
Average Collection Period	Win
Inventory Turn Over Ratio	Win
Times Interest Earned	Win
Return on Assets	Win
Return on Equity	Win

So, it looks like its Coke 3 and Pepsi 7. So, which company is better?

Whew! That was a lot of work! So, just looking at these numbers it might look like Pepsi is a better investment. But, you can't look at just the numbers, unless that is all you are interested in. There are some investors who are completely analytical. And that's fine! There is nothing wrong with that. If that is the kind of person you are, you have to be able to come up with an investment plan that uses this type of analysis.

Just for fun, I decided to add some financial information. If you look below, as of the dates stated you can see what activity the companies have had. It's pretty interesting isn't it?

As of July 10, 2008
Outstanding Shares

Coca-Cola	Pepsi
2.32B	1.59B

Market Cap.

Coca-Cola	Pepsi
$116.23B	$104.03B

Stock Price

Coca-Cola	Pepsi
$50.04/Sh	$65.59/Sh

As of August 20, 2008
Outstanding Shares

Coca-Cola	Pepsi
2.31B	1.57B

Market Cap.

Coca-Cola	Pepsi
$125.63B	$109.35B

Stock Price

Coca-Cola	Pepsi
$54.35/Sh	$69.85/Sh

If you come to the conclusion that fundamentals are an indication of where the stock should go, then you should not be surprised that Pepsi's stock price is higher than Coke's. Coke's market value, however, is higher. The market value is a simple calculation of multiplying the number of shares outstanding with the price of the stock at a given moment. In the case above, this information is based on the closing price as of the dates shown.

FORECASTING

You know, this is very important. The large companies use it all the time. The small companies rarely use it or use it to a small degree. Look at it this way, if the big companies use it, shouldn't you? Now, if you are a small company, I know what you are saying. "I'm a small company, with few employees, and we don't have time for these calculations." Or, "We don't understand the calculations or their meaning, so we don't bother with it." Well, you can think that way all you want, but I can say one thing with absolute certainty: Coca-Cola, Pepsi, Apple, General Motors, Microsoft, etc. all started out as small companies.

And they adopted the large company mentality and started thinking like large companies and adopted these practices. So, if you want to stay a small company, that's fine. If you want to become a big company, you are going to have to act like one.

The purpose of forecasting is to come up with an educated guess of what you expect to do in the upcoming year or years. Why do you need this? How can you plan for the next year without some guesses of where you want to be?

What do you expect for sales? Do you want or expect to increase sales by 10% or 20%? Do you want to expand your company? Do you want to create new divisions or diversify into new product lines? What do you want to do? This is going to get you energized and force you to think, and that's a great thing! You will be amazed at the ideas that come across your mind. When you get past the decision that you want to grow, your thought process changes as to how. How can I generate an additional 10% in sales? How can I enter that new market? That's when the fun begins. When your thinking changes along this line, there is something you are going to consider and that something is your competition. If your competition is smart, they are thinking about you. If you don't think Coca-Cola is thinking about Pepsi and Pepsi is thinking about Coca-Cola, you have been drinking too much soda pop.

In any event, the increase in sales, etc. will have an impact on your bottom line. That is, sales will have a direct and an indirect impact on your costs: direct labor, direct material, sales and administration, etc. If you don't have any idea about how much sales you want to have next year, how do you know how many people and in which departments you need to hire? I know a lot of companies hire by reaction. They start to see sales make a move up or they win a few big contracts and they start hiring a lot of people—only to have the sales drop off in the next few months. Then they have to lay off the people they just hired. There is a lot of planning that must take place for success.

OK, now you have decided you are going to move up the success ladder. Let's begin the process of forecasting.

There are a couple of forecasting methods. One of them is easy, but it is not that accurate. That is the Percentage of Sales Method. If you want a down-and-dirty forecast, try this. Take last year's income statement. Let's assume you want to increase sales by 15%. You put last year's numbers into a spread sheet and multiply all of the line items by 15%. That's quick, but not that accurate. You can expect direct material to rise by about that much. Direct material is directly related to the number of products produced. It's pretty much the same thing with direct labor. However, administration costs are not going to rise at the rate of 15%.

Typically, the same number of administrative people who were doing the work last year can do the same work this year. You may add a salesperson to reach your goals for the next year, but your analysis will tell if that is a wise move. But your accounting department isn't going to rise 15%. Your maintenance costs aren't going to rise 15%. Your utilities aren't going to rise 15%. That's why the Percentage Method, though quick, is not that accurate.

Now you could use this method and increase all of the costs by, say, 15%, for example. Then go back and analyze each account and input more realistic numbers in the line items that wouldn't increase by that amount.

In order to come up with a good forecast it is going to take a lot of work and time. That is why most small companies don't prepare them. Depending on the size of the company, the owner is also the salesperson, the bookkeeper, administrator, etc. This person doesn't have time to prepare a forecast.

We've already talked about this earlier in the book. Essentially, the more work, effort, and time you and your management team put into the forecast development the better the forecast.

Now, let's look at what kind of detail you need. Let's pick something easy.

Let's pretend you are a manufacturing organization and you make metal boxes for a cable company. All you make are the boxes, four sides made out of 18 gauge metal with holes drilled into the sides, etc.

Last year your company produced 1,000 boxes. Now, you are going to expand your sales and want to add another 500 boxes to the plan for a total of 1,500 boxes. There you go—you just created the sales forecast—1,500 boxes.

But wait, do you have to build 1,500 boxes to sell 1,500 boxes? Let's pretend you have 20 boxes left over from last year. The cost of those boxes (per box) is as follows:

Direct Labor:	$20
Direct Material:	$15
Overhead:	$10
Total:	$45

Total cost per box: $45 and there are 20 boxes left over so that gives us a total of $900 ($45/box multiplied by 20 boxes). Do you see how I came up with that? That is the value of the ending inventory last year and the beginning inventory this year.

So, we want to sell 1,500 boxes, we already have 20 boxes from last year, so we need to produce only 1,480 boxes, right? Wrong. If we produce the 1,480 boxes and sell the 20 boxes, we then meet our target of 1,500 boxes. But, what if we get another customer who wants an additional 50 boxes? We can't make the sale because we don't have any left. So we have to decide how much ending inventory we want to keep. Let's say we settle on 100 boxes of ending inventory. We had 20 boxes at the end of last year. The ending inventory gives you a cushion.

So, how much do we really need to produce?

Desired Ending Inventory	100
Plus: Expected Sales	1,500
Less: Beginning Inventory	(20)
Production Volume	**1,580**

So we have to produce 1,580 boxes to meet our goal of selling 1,500 and keep 100 in ending inventory and using the 20 in beginning inventory. How much will it cost in labor, material, and overhead to produce the 1,580 boxes?

Will it be the same cost as the beginning inventory? Probably not, we have to assume prices will rise. Employees will get raises, material costs will increase, etc. So, let's assume labor increases 5%, material costs rise 1%, and overhead rises 3%.

So in comparison to last year, let's look at some things.

Beginning Inventory Costs	
Direct Labor	$20.00
Number of Boxes	20
Direct Labor Costs	**$400.00**
Direct Material	$15.00
Number of Boxes	20
Direct Material Costs	**$300.00**
Overhead	$10.00
Number of Boxes	20
Direct Overhead Costs	**$200.00**
Total Beginning Inventory Costs	$900.00
Production Inventory Costs	
Direct Labor + 5% Cost Increase	$21.00
Number of Boxes	1,580
Direct Labor Costs	**$33,180.00**

Direct Material + 10% Cost Increase	$16.50
Number of Boxes	1,580
Direct Material Costs	**$26,070.00**

Overhead + 3% Increase	$10.30
Number of Boxes	1,580
Direct Overhead Costs	**$16,274.00**

| Total Production Costs | $75,524.00 |

Ending Inventory Costs
Direct Labor + 5% Cost Increase	$21.00
Number of Boxes	100
Direct Labor Costs	**$2,100.00**

Direct Material + 10% Cost Increase	$16.50
Number of Boxes	100
Direct Material Costs	**$1,650.00**

Overhead + 3% Increase	$10.30
Number of Boxes	100
Direct Overhead Costs	**$1,030.00**

| Total Ending Inventory Costs | $4,780.00 |

The cost breakdown is as follows:
Costs of Goods Sold
Beginning Inventory	$900
Production Sold	$70,744
Total Costs of Goods Sold	**$71,644**

So, here is what it looks like. The beginning inventory of 20 boxes is worth or costs $900. To build the additional 1,580 boxes will cost $75,524. Ending inventory is $4,780. Now, we will sell 1,500 boxes out of our inventory. The cost of the 1,500 boxes sold is $71,644, which includes 20 boxes from the beginning inventory and 1,480 boxes from production. That will leave us with 100 boxes in our inventory that has an associated cost of $4,780.00.

Let's move on to general administrative expense.

For the most part, general administrative expenses don't change too much for such a small increase in sales. General administrative expenses include things like office salaries, maintenance, utilities, etc. If sales increase 10%, the trash pickup isn't going to increase 10%. So, for our purposes, let's say the general administrative expenses stay the same.

So, here is our pro forma income statement:

Sales	$120,000
Less: Cost of Goods Sold	($71,644)
Gross Profit	**$48,356**
Less: General Admin	($25,000)
Net Profit	**$23,356**

This is a very, very simple pro forma income statement. The purpose of it is to give you an idea of how they are prepared.

Usually, annual sales are not spread evenly over the year. What I mean is that if you expect to sell $120,000 next year, it probably won't come in at exactly $10,000 increments per month. Wouldn't that make planning easy! There is fluctuation that can be caused by seasonal sales, for example. As well as sales fluctuating through the year, your variable costs will fluctuate. However, your fixed costs won't. I have developed a spread sheet that shows how the costs would be determined how the cash flow. Unfortunately, this book isn't large enough to display it. If you are interested in seeing it, you can email me at: dean@dbrownjr.com and I will email it to you.

Pro formas and budgets are imperative. It doesn't matter the size of your company; you need to put these together. Going through the thought process helps you identify weaknesses and strengths. You might discover that you don't have enough funds for the project. It's better to know now instead of halfway through the project and then panic when you run out of cash.

It also helps you to take a hard look at your business and how you run it. In addition, it helps you take a hard look at your competitors! What they do or don't do will have a profound impact on your success.

There are lots of reasons why companies don't put together budgets: they take too much time, the figures are worthless by the time they make their way down to finalization and implementation, those responsible for the budgets didn't participate in creating them, and so on. That's why budgets need to be based on strategic plans of the organization! And those strategic plans need to be communicated to those down the organization chain. In addition, allow, encourage, and require departments to have input into the budget process. This will get you the "buy in" it desperately needs from the organization and from all management levels of the organization. Google "financial budgeting" and you'll get a lot of great information to hone your skills.

Whew! We got through that! Now let's look at working capital.

WORKING CAPITAL

Working capital is just that, capital (money) you have to work with. Primarily, working capital is for managing the current assets and current liabilities.

With this capital you are going to purchase raw material, pay for direct labor, pay salaries, buy office supplies, pay other expenses, make the Lamborghini payment (the company car, of course), etc.

Working capital is a key part of the production forecast and budgeting. The production forecast will tell you how much money you need to finance production and run the company. With this we can work out how much we are going to receive from accounts receivable that was generated from sales. So knowing how much money is coming in and going out, by month, we know how much money in excess and shortage we will be dealing with. So, for those months we are short of cash, what do we do?

Hopefully, prior to the need for cash we have obtained a line of credit. This is credit that our bank has given us that we can use when we need it and pay it back when the cash situation turns positive. Small companies will have small lines of credit. For example, they may have a line of credit of $1,000,000. Big companies can have a $30,000,000–$100,000,000 line of credit. Remember, it is not another checking account to write checks off of. No, this is an account you tap into when you need it and pay it back as fast as possible. It's best to apply for and get a line of credit before you actually need it. You don't want to have a bad situation and then go to your banker and get a line of credit. You probably won't get it. Banks like to lend you money when you don't need it.

Lines of credit are key in business. The large companies have them so believe that small companies should have them. It would be hard for a company to accept the opportunity of a large job (larger than usual) and try to finance it internally. If you are starting a business or have one established, talk to your banker about a line of credit, even if you don't need one. It's better to have and not need than to need and not have.

I know this one guy who started a commercial fire sprinkler business. It was a small company that secured a $1,000,000 line of credit. After doing that, the business took off. Instead of limiting bids to one-story commercial projects, the company was able to expand and propose multifloor projects...and win them. The guy said he couldn't have risen to the sales volume that he eventually generated without the line of credit.

Cash Management. Now that we have the line of credit squared away let's move on to some ways to bring cash in quicker. First let's take a look at e-commerce. E-commerce is great way to do business. Customers log on to your Web site, purchase your product, and pay by credit card or PayPal. Within seconds you have completed the purchase and received payment. That is a lot better than waiting for a check to come in.

I remember reading how Amazon.com was capitalizing on this. I'm sure you know about Amazon.com. I would assume that all of their transactions or just about all of them are credit or debit card transactions. So, when you log on to the Web site and purchase a product, you use your credit card and charge the funds to your credit card that day or definitely the next day. Amazon turns around and orders the book from the wholesaler or retailer. The retailer turns around and sends the book to you. Amazon pays the retailer according to the agreement, which is probably thirty days from purchase, unless the discount is taken. But what if you have to accept checks? This is when lockboxes come in.

Let's say you have a company that is headquartered in Denver, Colorado, USA. It's a pretty good-size company and you have operations, etc. all over the United States, Africa, Europe, Canada, and South America. How can you get money from your customers into your bank account as fast as possible?

You would establish banking relations in each of the designated cities you identify. This is probably with the help of your bank. At each of these banks you have a lockbox with a local address for that lock box. For example, a lockbox in Chicago, Illinois, would have a Chicago address. One in Germany or Italy would have one there. The same thing goes for South America. Now, when your South American customer pays an invoice, the customer sends it to a South American address that is located at a bank. The bank will process the check and forward the funds to the headquarter bank in Denver. Basically, that is how lockboxes work.

There is a wise way to improve your collection of funds. This will probably sound crazy, but a good way to improve collections and cash flow is to not take on a customer that has a high probability of not paying. OK, how do you know that a company has a high probability of not paying? Get a Dunn & Bradstreet report on the company. A Dunn & Bradstreet report is like a corporate credit rating. Basically, companies send their financial statements to Dunn & Bradstreet, they review and analyze them and give them a rating...like an AAA rating. You call up Dunn & Bradstreet to get a corporate rating on a potential customer. They will tell you what it is and then you make the decision to do business with that company. If you don't like the potential customer's rating or it makes you nervous, instead of creating a credit account, you make them pay COD (cash on delivery), until they establish credit with you. However, if you do this, you probably won't get the customer, unless they are desperate for your product or service. Sometimes, turning down a potential customer for financial reasons can be a profitable decision. The loss of potential revenue may be better than the gain in potential headaches trying to collect.

Regardless of the rating, you make the final decision to do business with the potential customer or how you will do business with them. Bear in mind, I'm sure there is a story behind every bad rating. Who knows what happened to or with the customer to obtain a bad rating? Yes, there are some entities that are poorly run and their operations and payment history proves it. There are others that might have had an event beyond their control that caused them to fall behind and subsequently get a bad rating. It is your call.

Another major cash drain is inventory. Properly managed, inventory can be managed, but mismanaged inventory will cause you problems.

You have a manager who finds a great bargain on some steel. The manager buys enough steel to last you three months, but at what cost? Three months of cost (cash out the door) that's what. So you have drained your bank account and now it will take you three months to recoup that investment. Sure, it was less expensive, but you may have to tap your line of credit or put off paying some vendors because of the lack of cash.

SHORT TERM FINANCING

Let's look at some ways to finance your business. These are short term ways. Probably the two most popular ways are a line of credit and accounts payable.

The line of credit is what we already talked about. You must pay particular attention to it, because it can run away from you. This service isn't free. There are charges associated with it. I know one bank that charges a certain percentage, but if you don't use the line of credit the percentage rate is lower. Stop! I know what you are thinking. I'm going to establish a line of credit and the bank is going to encourage me not to use it? The answer is yes.

The second one is accounts payable. You probably didn't know it, but that is a temporary loan for about thirty days. Here is how it works as a short term loan. Let's pretend this is November 1, 20XX. You purchase product from your vendor. The vendor turns around and invoices you with payment due in thirty days. Guess what, you have the product and you don't have to pay for it for thirty days. Now you can use those goods to build or resell your product and hopefully, sell it all before you have to pay your vendor. If that's the case then you used the vendor's money to make your money. Now that is using other people's money!

Still another form of short term financing is accounts receivable factoring. That is when a company sells its receivables. A lot of start-up companies use this to help get them through tough times. By no means do you want to use this on a constant basis. It is incredibly expensive in terms of the percentage rate. The rate can be as high as 25%. Factoring companies prefer the newest or youngest (when thinking about accounts receivable aging), because there is a higher probability of collecting them. Some will buy your older ones, i.e., ninety days and older, but they may put a clause in the contract that says if they can't collect in a certain amount of time that you have to buy it back. This reduces their risk and increases yours.

TIME VALUE OF MONEY

OK, let's talk a little about the time value of money. I know a lot of you out there are asking why you need to bother learning this when Excel spreadsheets and calculators can do it easily. You are right; they can do it easier than paper and pencil. We are not going to spend a lot of time on it; I just want to cover some basics. The first thing I am going to assume is that you are aware of the formulas for present value, future value, and annuities. If not, you can Google them or find a finance textbook.

Money has a value that is related to time and interest/discount rates. If you own a house, think about your mortgage. Do you own a car; think about your auto loan.

The time value of money is incredibly valuable when you are looking at investing in something or determining if a long-term project is financially viable.

Our first example will be on Present Value. We are not going to show how it works with building or buying a plant or anything like that. We're going to talk about golf. Before we do that, I want to explain something. Regarding the time value of money, it is important to know when the transaction will take place, either the first of the month or the end of the month. There is a difference, since if it takes place the first of the month, there is more interest. Do you remember when you bought a house? Part of your closing costs was determined what day you closed on. If it was close to the first of the month the costs were higher due to more interest incurred. It's the same thing here. However for our purposes, we will assume that the transactions will take place on the last day of the month.

In the summer of 2007 Tiger Woods won the FEDEX championship and part of his winnings was $10,000,000, put into a retirement account that he can't access until he is forty-five years old. So, let's figure out how much the PGA would have had to deposit on December 31, 2007, to accumulate $10,000,000 by the time Tiger reaches forty-five years old.

For the sake of math, let's assume Tiger was thirty years old on December 31, 2007. How much would the PGA have had to deposit on that date, and not deposit any more, to achieve a balance of $10,000,000 by this time fifteen years later? Let's assume an interest rate of 5%. Where did I get it from…I just pulled it out of the air. I could have tied it to the current prime rate or something like that. In any given case, that number will supplied to you for whatever reason.

The formula for present value is:

Present Value = Future Value x $(1/(1 + \text{interest rate})^{\text{number of periods}}$

Now that we have the formula, let's drop in the data that we know. I'll just rewrite the formula with the data.

Present Value = $10,000,000 x $(1/(1 + 5\%)^{15}$

Present Value = $10,000,000 x $(1/(1.05)^{15}$

Present Value = $10,000,000 x $1/(2.0789)$

Present Value = $10,000,000 x .48102

Present Value = $4,810,236. If the PGA deposits $4,810,236 today AND earns an average of 5% each year for fifteen years, they will have Tiger's money waiting for him.

What if the interest rate is 4%? How much will they need then?

Present Value = $10,000,000 x $(1/(1 + 4\%)^{15}$

Present Value = $10,000,000 x $(1/(1.04)^{15}$

Present Value = $10,000,000 x $1/(1.800)$

Present Value = $10,000,000 x .5555

Present Value = $5,555,555 at 4%

What if the interest rate is 6%?

Present Value = $10,000,000 x $(1/(1 + 6\%)^{15}$

Present Value = $10,000,000 x $(1/(1.06)^{15}$

Present Value = $10,000,000 x 1/(2.396)

Present Value = $10,000,000 x .4173

Present Value = $4,173,622 at 6%

Now, let's evaluate all three together:

#1 Present Value = $4,810,236 at 5%
#2 Present Value = $5,555,555 at 4%
#3 Present Value = $4,173,622 at 6%

Take a look at the three. Do you see that as the interest rate goes down, you have to start out with more and as the interest rate goes up, you start out with less? Why? This is where "time" comes in. In all three examples, the time needed is fifteen years. In example #2, you are earning 4% for fifteen years and in example #3 you are earning 6% for fifteen years. You are earning more per year and therefore you need less to start with.

Now, let's look at how interest works with an income stream or what is called an annuity.

Let's assume you are reviewing a project you want to invest in that will generate a certain amount of money every year for the next five years. Is it worth it, today, to invest in that project?

Look at it this way. You are the chief financial officer for a company. The chief executive officer comes to you and is thinking about investing in a company. The CEO wants to know if it is a good idea. Now, I'm going to make this very simple; however, be aware that it can become very complicated. But for our purposes, we'll keep it simple.

Let's create the example. You expect the investment to generate $100,000 per year for five years. The current interest rate is 8%. After five years you will reevaluate the investment. So, you are willing to invest $500,000 in the company.

The formula is the same one as above, in the Tiger Woods example, but for each year we are receiving money.

On the surface here is what the investment income looks like this:

Year(s)	Income
Year 1:	$100,000
Year 2:	$100,000
Year 3:	$100,000
Year 4:	$100,000
Year 5:	$100,000
Total Income Received:	**$500,000**

How much would this investment cost in today's dollars?

To make this easy, I am going to assume you have access to an Excel spreadsheet or a financial calculator. You can calculate these figures so much faster than by hand. I'm just displaying it in this manner so you can see it.

Ok we know we have $100,000 income per year and the interest rate for all five years is eight percent. Now, even though the interest rate says the same per year, the effect on each year is different. Why? Because the farther out a year from today, the more interest it can be assumed it would make.

So, for the Year 1, the $100,000 multiplied by the factor .9259 $(1/(1.08)^1)$ would equal $92,590. In

Year 2, the $100,000 multiplied by the factor .8573 $(1/(1.08)^2)$ would equal $85,733. If you continue to calculate the years and add up the present values, you will get a total present value of $399,223. In other words, the value of the investment that pays you $100,000 per year at 8% interest is worth $399,223 today.

This is the long written version, but there is an equation that will let you derive the answer quickly. There are four tables that you can find on the Internet or in a finance book. The four tables are: Present Value, Present Value Annuity, Future Value, and Future Value Annuity. With these tables you can just about calculate anything that required the time value of money, but Excel or a financial calculator is so much easier and faster

So, based on this example, the present value of an income producing stream that is generating $100,000 per year for five years is worth $399,223 at 8% interest or discount rate. Is that good or bad? That depends on the interest rate or discount rate; is it good or bad? Also, it may depend on the return on investment of other potential projects. Also, you have to consider your expectations.

If the current interest rate is 10% that is not good. You'll be earning 8% when you could be earning

10%. What if the interest rate is 6%? That would be good, because you would be earning 8% when you could be earning 6%. There are other factors to consider as well. Could you invest in something better that might give you a better return? A return, not necessarily in dollars, but in ecological quality, human resources, etc. should be considered. A lot of thought has to go into it.

Now, let's assume you want to build a plant or invest in a new product line and you need extra cash. You could sell corporate bonds to raise the funds you need. Now, this is for bigger companies, so I am just giving you an example, in case you ever run across it.

OK, you need $1,000,000. You are going to sell $1,000,000 worth of corporate bonds paying 10% interest for the next twenty years. The interest is paid at the end of December of every year.

As an investor, I am going to consider the cost and return. Let's assume that this is a healthy company and the risk of default is very small.

As an investor, here is what I am going to receive over a period of time.

We are going to use the same analysis as above, but instead we are going to use the formula instead of listing the amount each year. However, there is a twist. With corporate bonds or bonds in general, the investor receives the interest payment each year and then at the end of the year the investor gets the principal amount. This is one form of a corporate bond structure. So, I am investor, I buy a $1,000,000 corporate bond paying 10%. I would receive $100,000 (10% x $1,000,000) every year in December. Then at the end of twenty years, I would get $1,000,000. So, how much am I willing to pay for this. Let's do the math.

There are two parts to this equation: 1) we have to calculate the net present value of the annual payments and 2) we have to calculate the net present value of the final $1,000,000 payment.

First let's calculate the net present value of the annual payments. I'm going to use the formula:

$$PVoa = PMT((1-(1/(1 + i)^{20}))/i)$$

$$PVoa = \$100,000((1-(1/(1.10^{)20})/.10)$$

$$PVoa = \$100,000(1-.1486)/.10$$

$$PVoa = \$100,000 \times 8.5135 = \$851,356.$$

Now the calculation for the net present value of the $1,000,000 final payment.

$1,000,000 x $1/(1+.10)^{20}$ which equals: $1,000,000 x $1/6.727 = $1,000,000 x .1486 = $148,600.

We add the two together and we get $999,956. So, we would have to pay $999,956, or $1,000,000, for the bond. Now you might be saying why would I pay $1,000,000 for a $1,000,000 bond? Actually, you are paying $1,000,000 that is paying you $100,000 per year for twenty years and then $1,000,000 at the end of the period.

Now that we know how much our project is going to cost, how are we going to finance it? Good question!

First let's look at our sources of financing. A lot of this depends on the size and financial status of your company.

First: Bank loans. You can go to your banker and request a loan. The banker will ask you to fill out an application and supply the most current audited or reviewed financial statements. Subsequent to that, the banker may ask you to sign a personal guarantee, guaranteeing that you (the guarantor) guarantee the loan and if the company defaults, you will be held liable. This is not always good, but sometimes desperation requires it. I knew a guy who personally guaranteed for some very expensive equipment that his company bought. There were some business problems that led to much larger problems and the company went out of business. The bank went to the guarantor for payment and, since his company went under, he couldn't make the payments either. So, he had to sell his house to make the payment. I also know another owner of a company who absolutely refuses to sign personal guarantees for the very reason I just talked about.

If bankers don't ask for a personal guarantee, they may ask to pledge collateral to support the loan. This is very common. Recently, history was made when Ford Motor Company pledged the Ford logo (the blue oval that says Ford) as collateral. No one ever tried pledging a trademark name.

Second: You could go to the stock market and issue common stock. The advantage is that you could bring in a lot of money if you have a good plan and the business economic conditions are right. The disadvantages are that you have to generate quarterly and annual Securities Exchange Commission reports, pacify shareholders, look over you shoulder for someone buying your stock for a friendly or unfriendly takeover, etc. Just the quarterly and annual filings can be quite expensive. In addition, if you are issuing additional stock you have to worry about diluting your current shareholders' holdings.

Third: Issue corporate bonds, another form of corporate IOUs. The corporate bonds still require some Securities Exchange Commission filing, but not to the extent of common stock filing.

Fourth: Fund it internally with the checking account.

Fifth: There are others, such as issuing preferred stock, etc., but for the sake of the purposes of this book, we won't go into preferred stock.

Now, even though these are ways of bringing in capital, there is still an associated cost that must be reckoned with. With bank loans there is interest. If it is a compensating bank loan then you have interest on top of the minimum funds set aside.

For common stock and corporate bond issues there is the cost of floating the issues. Nothing in life is free and raising capital is no different.

You have to look at the cost of each individual item when deciding on which avenues and how to mix the methods of raising capital.

Look at it this way and assume the following:

To borrow funds, the best interest rate you can get is 8%.

Let's say the cost of issuing common stock is 10%.

You might say that it is easy to just borrow what you need to finance the project. Yes, that would be easy, but remember banks may not lend you all of the money you need, because of your financial situation. If the banks don't give you all of the money, you may have to go to the equity markets and bond markets to get the rest.

Each of the items I mentioned has an associated cost and whatever you raise from each source will determine your overall or weighted cost. This is important when determining whether to proceed with a project.

"Mix" refers to the mixture of preferred stock, common stock, and debt, the three forms of financing. All three of these carry different costs. In addition to the costs, we have to consider that in certain economic times it may better to apply more to one category than another. Here is what I mean. When you have an economic situation where interest rates are low, you might be able to fund the whole project with debt. The advantage is that you don't have to issue more stock and subsequently pay for the issue and dilute the other shareholders. When times are reversed, it may be cheaper to issue more common stock. So, it depends on what is facing you at that moment in time.

Now it is logical to assume that in order for you to be profitable every project should have a profit percentage that is in excess of the cost of capital. For example, if your weighted cost of capital is 10%, and you are considering a project that has a return of, say, 15%, you would probably, for all intents and purposes, give it the "green light." On the other side, if you have the same weighted cost of capital of 10% and you are considering a project that is expected to generate 10% or even 9% return on investment, you would probably pass on it. Or should you? There isn't any law that says you have to pass on it. Really, it would be wise to look at the whole picture.

Let's say this 10% profit—10% weighted average cost of capital project—was actually a foothold into a new market or was a backbone infrastructure to something bigger. Then your subject projects could possibly generate much more revenue, because of the foundation(s) that have been laid. So, don't throw away a project, purely on numbers. Look at the whole project and how it meets the company's goals and objectives.

RISK

Now that we have done all that, there is something very, very important that we have to cover. That topic is risk!

How do you define risk? It's all relative. Some investors invest in commodities and are not affected by the risk; others are. Some investors "short" stocks and options and are not affected by the risk. Others are risk averse; they want to play it as safe as possible. I know something about risk. I have traded commodities, currencies, and I was a day trader for about six months. Because of the size of my account, risk was important to me. When I was day-trading I was a basket case. I had my computer set up at work to start beeping when certain prices were met, either for or against me. Then I would minimize the screen while I was working. Then when the bells started sounding I would drop everything and take appropriate action. Well, one time I was talking with my boss in my office and the bells starting going off. I knew something was happening, but I didn't think it would be a good career move to cut my boss off and look at the trade. Now you are probably asking, why was I trading commodities while at work? Well, that's a fair question, but I had permission from my bosses.

What kind of risk do you like? I call this the "Sleep Factor." In other words, what amount of risk can you sleep with at night? As I said, I day-traded the E-mini S&P 500. Even though I was out of the market at the end of each day, I was a basket case at night, because I didn't know what I was going to do the next day or if I was going to make any money. I used to day-trade commodities and the same thing happened. One day I was standing in the coffee line at the local coffee shop. My commodities broker called about a trade in cotton that we had spoken about the previous night. We agreed to go long on the cotton. There was a hurricane coming to the southeast coast and the thought was that it would damage the cotton crops and the demand and the price would rise. This call took place at 7:25 a.m. mountain standard time. The market opened at 7:30 a.m. We agreed to set the stop at $500. The stop is the maximum I was willing to lose if the trade went wrong. I got my coffee and sat down. It was 7:35 a.m. My broker called me up and congratulated me because I just lost $500. That is a record for me. One record I never want to break. See what I mean by risk? You can't get mad. It wasn't personal, just business. As a result, I had to adjust my trading styles, markets, and philosophies to accommodate my risk tolerance. You have to do the same thing!

The next question is how can you limit your risk? Let's face it; you can't make it go away 100%! You can reduce it substantially, but at the same time, you reduce your potential income. As they say, no guts – no glory.

When dealing with corporate projects, etc., how can you place a risk on that? You don't have any third-party organizations that can evaluate your situation and give you a report. Here you have to rely on the advice of you staff. These people are a great source of information and should be trusted...assuming you haven't squandered their bonus for this year.

Your employees have a pretty good pulse on the customers, manufacturing capabilities, etc. Gather the right personnel in the room at the same time to lay everything on the table, the pros and cons, limitations, probabilities, etc. You can come up with a probability factor of the potential of the project's success. Is the probability the risk? Is a 70% probability of success less risky than, say 40%? Not necessarily. You could be entering a new market, which, based on all of your research, shows you will have a 70% chance of success. That sounds good, except that you have never done anything like this before and no one on your staff has either. So now what is the risk?

When dealing with investing in stocks, you have something you can look at called "beta" or "beta coefficient." It is calculated using regression analysis and estimates the reaction of a stock to the overall market. The S&P 500 is considered a beta of 1. So, that is the benchmark. When reviewing a stock's beta you can compare with 1.00 or the S&P 500. Most technical stocks that are traded on the NASDAQ have a beta greater than 1. So, if a stock has a beta greater than 1, such as 1.20, this means that the stock is approximately 20% more risky than the S&P 500. A riskier stock has a ying and yang attitude. Yes, for the most part, it can generate more profits quicker or generate more losses quicker.

On the other side of the coin you have the same situation with the long-standing stocks like Coca-Cola, General Electric, etc. Their betas are less than 1.0. They are considered less risky and therefore, have the potential to deliver less than exciting returns. But…you might be able to sleep better at night.

So, do you like traveling at Mach 1 with your hair on fire or do you like to cruise in your favorite Bentley with the top down?

LONG TERM DEBT AND LEASE FINANCING

We're going to talk a little about long term debt and lease financing. As we have said, debt is a double-edged sword. Some is good, but too much is not good.

First you have secured and unsecured debt. Secured debt is backed by something that has been put up as collateral. It is secured by something. Look at it this way, you buy a house. You take out a mortgage, what does the house become? It becomes collateral.

If the company cannot make the payments the lending institution seizes the collateral. Unsecured debt doesn't have any collateral to support it. So, why would an investor want it? Usually, the company has to offer a higher premium or interest rate to attract investors. The higher premium or interest rate is "bonus" for accepting more risk than usual.

From there, we will go to senior and junior debt. In the event a company does not meet its financial obligations and there is consideration of selling assets to pay off debt, the senior debt holders will have first claim to proceeds from the assets before junior debt holders.

So, if you plan on buying another company's debt, know where you stand in the hierarchy of who will get paid first in the worst possible situation.

For the most part, bond interest rates stay the same for the term of the bond. However, with floating rate bonds, the interest rate does basically what the title says—it floats with market conditions. With these types of bonds, you are assured of earning a fair market rate on interest.

LEASING

Leasing is a form of a liability. There are two kinds of leasing: operation and capital leases. They are treated differently, for accounting purposes, and therefore show up differently on the financial statements. Operational leases are short term leases and they are expensed in the financial statements. Typically, these leases are for copiers, autos, etc. As I said earlier, they are expensed in the financial statements and don't have any presence on the balance sheet. Capital leases are treated differently. The mind-set you should take is that even though a capital lease asset is truly owned by the lessee, based on the definition, it shows up on the company's balance sheet as an asset and a liability and it is amortized over the life of the lease.

DIVIDENDS

Let's take a look at dividends and how important they are. Remember, the issuance of dividends is a way of rewarding the investor for being patient with management's operational success. Usually, when companies begin their operations, they haven't had enough financial success to reward investors with dividends. The way investors have been rewarded is with the increase of the stock price. Now, after the company has become successful, management can distribute dividends.

Is it a requirement for companies to pay dividends? No, they can pay them when they want. Take a look at Microsoft. In January of 2003, Microsoft announced that they would pay an annual dividend to shareholders for the first time. The annual divided would be payable on March 7 of that year, to those on record as of February 21 of the same year.

Prior to this Microsoft never distributed dividends. Now, why would a company the size of Microsoft, which has that mountain of cash available, resolve not to pay dividends? Maybe, there is a reason. Maybe, they know something that the outside investor doesn't know. Maybe, they have plans for the cash that they perceive will generate a higher return or be better for the company than giving it to the shareholders.

If you remember at that time, Microsoft was being sued by a lot of outside parties. Maybe Microsoft perceived that the litigations were possibly coming to the end and a settlement was in sight and they needed the cash for it. Maybe they had their eyes on some acquisitions. Maybe they had some internal investments that they were considering. All in all, Microsoft deemed it in the best interest of the company to keep the funds close at hand to deal with some pending situations. Obviously, this is to the angst of investors who would love to get their hands on some dividend cash, but that's business. Don't like it, sell the stock or try to buy a major stake of stock in the company and push out management.

Let's go over some important dates to consider. Declaration Date, this is the date that the board of directors announces to the world that the company will pay a dividend. The Ex-Dividend Date, is the last date the stock trades before the dividend. The Date of Record is the date that the company looks at the records to see who the shareholders are. An investor must be listed as a holder of record on this date. Date of Payment, is the date the company sends out the checks.

Stock Dividends are issued when a company would much rather reward investors with stock instead of cash. For example, a company has ten shareholders and each owns 100,000 shares of the company. The stock is at $100 per share. Thus 100,000 shares multiplied by $100/share gives the company a market value of $10,000,000. The company declares a 10% stock dividend. Here is what is going to happen. Before the dividend there are 1,000,000 shares (10 shareholders x 100,000 shares each) outstanding. Subsequent to the dividend there will be issued an additional 100,000 shares (1,000,000 multiplied by 10%). This brings the total of outstanding shares to 1,100,000 (1,000,000 original outstanding plus 100,000 additional shares from the stock dividend). So how many shares do the ten owners own now? There are a total 1,110,000 shares outstanding and the same ten owners. Now each owner will share in the stock dividend distribution so, their shares owned will rise from 100,000 to 110,000. Do you see how that happened? Now the question looms, what happens to the market value? Does it go up by 10% also? The answer is no. The only thing that happened was more stock certificates were printed and issued. So, if the market value doesn't change, what happens to the stock price? It will go down, watch.

The stock was $100 per share when there were 100,000 outstanding shares and the market value was $10,000,000. We know the market value stays the same and the new outstanding shares are 110,000, so the new stock price is $90.91 per share. In other words, you take the same market value of $10,000,000 and divide it by the new outstanding shares of 110,000 and you get $90.91 per share. Now the owners still own 10% (110,000 per shareholder divided by 1,100,000 equates to 10%). So, their holdings were not diluted, but the price dropped approximately 10% ($90.91/share divided by $100/share). Do you see that?

So, what's the big deal about stock dividends? Well, investors can walk away with different stories. Here are two possibilities. If a company wants to issue stock dividends, does that mean the company doesn't have the funds for a cash dividend? Is the company trying to hide inadequate cash flow? Also, if there are a lot of shareholders, this is an easy way to drop the price of the stock. This also enables long-term shareholders to increase their holdings without investing another dime, euro or rupee.

Typically stock dividends are in the 10% range. This brings us to stock splits. Stock splits are a form of a stock dividend on steroids. Instead of 10%, the range for stock splits is in the 20%–25% range. It will have the same effect on the stock price and shareholder distribution, but on a bigger scale. So, there isn't really too much to get excited about when it comes to stock splits. Your percentage of ownership is still the same, the market value is still the same, the stock price has been proportionally adjusted, and you own more shares. That may be a good thing for your ego though. You end up owning a lot more shares.

Sometimes the company will buy back or repurchase its stock. This has a positive effect on the earnings per share, because there are fewer shares, which may excite the shareholders.

Now that we have that down. We have analyzed parts of the financial statements; now look at how we analyze the financial statements as a whole.

READING FINANCIAL STATEMENTS

Let's take a look at how to read financial statements. This is imperative, because you will be able to understand your department or company better.

I personally knew a man who owned a number of manufacturing companies. He wasn't an accountant or even a finance person. Previous to owning his own businesses, he was a vice president of a large company. However, he could read and understand financial statements.

There are a number of methods you can use to analyze financial statements. However, for our purposes, we want to review some methods that are quick and easy.

There are two methods I like the best. It's up to you to decide which one is better. You determine which one suits your purposes and gives you a comfort feel.

Method one is easy. What you do is take the two periods you are analyzing, monthly, quarterly, or annually. You bring up both periods you are analyzing side by side.

Let's assume you are a electronics company. You can compare this month's activity to last month's or last year's. Here is an example: You revenue for May 2004 is $255,043 and April 2004 is $245,908. That is a positive variance of $12,134. It is positive because this month's revenue is larger than last month's.

You can do the same thing with expenses. May telephone expenses were $1,800 and the previous month (April) was $2,400. That is a positive variance of $600, because the expenses are less than the previous month.

You can do this for every account. Now, you might not want to analyze every variance. Some are too small to worry about. So use your discretion.

Now, take the difference between the two periods.
Then you take a look at the differences. Review and
analyze the large differences. Should you develop
a minimum variance that guarantees reviewing of
an account? You could, but it would be determined
by the size of your company. What I mean is that
for some companies, a variance of $2,000 is large.
Microsoft would lose that in rounding. So, it is
relative.

OK, for the above example, let's say that you are
going to review every variance that exceeds $2,000.
What I like to do is pull up the detail for that account.
I view every dollar amount in the detail and check
to see that each amount can be verified and agreed
to. It could be that there is something wrong with
the transaction; it could be incorrectly coded, etc. If
every amount is verified, then you have to take a look
at what actually happened. Maybe something went
wrong and you had to replace a part or something.
Just make sure you can justify what the amounts are
or why. This gives you a view of what is going on and
a plan on how to recover. Now, I must warn you. Even
though you know what happened, you can explain
it, and maybe even justify it, it doesn't mean your
boss will be happy.

Even though you may have come up with a minimum
review figure, it doesn't mean you should ignore
every amount that is under. Still, take a quick look

at the others, but make a conscious decision to pass on reviewing. For example, you may have a standard monthly payment such as rent. Well, the variance between the two should be zero. But with a quick scan, if you see a variance, even though it is less than the $2,000 you agreed upon as a minimum, it would be noteworthy to review it. Maybe the rent went up. Maybe you are being charged for some repairs or something like that. It is just additional information you need to run your business or department.

OK, you are looking at the expenses, but the same thing goes for sales. Roberto Goizueta, the former CEO of Coca-Cola, once said, "I don't like surprises, not even good ones." Let's deviate a little bit. Some of you may think that an unexpected jump in sales is good, but is it? Yes, on the surface it is. You have more income to pay bills, maybe give out some dearly promised bonuses, maybe look at expansion. The reason it might not be good is that, if you didn't plan for the increase, you didn't "plan" for the additional cost. Now some of your current costs may not support the unexpected revenue. For example, you may not have expected the increase and now you are scrambling, looking for additional direct labor to hire and maybe additional material supplies. If you can't find the labor, you may have to pay overtime. That is an unexpected expense! The same thing goes for cash; if you didn't expect it you may not have forecast for the increase in cash use and now you have to increase your credit line to support the growth. So, yes, additional sales are good, planned additional sales are better.

Now, let's take a look at the other method.

This one has a cumulative average effect. It works pretty well, but takes a little more work. For example, let's say I am analyzing a electronics company. The current month's revenue is $286,129. The year-to-date revenue for six months is $1,797,679. So, how can I analyze this? Since this is for the six months, year-to-date, I will divide the $1,797,697 by 6 months and get $299,616 per month. Now, I can compare the six month average with the current month's figure. The difference between $299,616 and $286,129 is ($13,487). That is a negative number which is not good for sales. What it means is that current month's sales are lower than the six month average by $13,487. Now if this number is insignificant, because this is the beginning of the slow period, you might not do any research. If this is out of character, than you might want to look into it and see what caused it. Maybe, a trend is developing and this way you can catch it quickly.

You can do the same thing for expenses. Let's take a look at office salaries – current month $18,4166 and six month total is $167,931. Let's assume we have all ready performed the calculations and we come up with the following: The six month average is $27,988 and the current' month's salaries are $18,416. The variance is $9,572. Now that is a positive variance, because actuals are less than the six month average. Now that's good!

Now don't get the negative/positive variances mixed up between revenue figures and expense/cost figures. A negative variance in revenue is not good; the current month is less than the average. A negative variance is good in the expense/cost categories, because the current month costs are less than the six month average.

Now what you do is create your own cheat sheet. You print out the income statement. Perform the calculations above for each account. For those that require analysis, to the right of the number write down a few words to describe the variance. For example, 75% of the advertising negative variance is due to increased advertising for new product. Or something like that. I think you get my meaning. Now if you really want to blow some minds, don't write it down. Memorize it! Then when you are in the meeting and you rattling off figures and explanations with out looking at anything they will think you know your business!

OK, that's about it for this class. There is a lot more, but for what you need in the short term, this should do it.

If you have any questions, send me an e-mail: dean@ dbrownjr.com or visit www.finance-accounting101.com.

May you succeed at all you put your hand to.

Class dismissed.

APPENDIX

Pepsi Balance Sheet and Income Statement

Pepsi Balance Sheet

PEPSI
Balance Sheet

All numbers in thousands

PERIOD ENDING	29-Dec-07
Cash And Cash Equivalents	910,000
Short Term Investments	1,571,000
Net Receivables	4,389,000
Inventory	2,290,000
Other Current Assets	991,000
Total Current Assets	**10,151,000**
Long Term Investments	4,475,000
Property Plant and Equipment	11,228,000
Goodwill	5,169,000
Intangible Assets	2,044,000
Accumulated Amortization	-
Other Assets	1,356,000

Deferred Long Term Asset Charges	205,000
Total Assets	**34,628,000**
Accounts Payable	6,209,000
Short/Current Long Term Debt	-
Other Current Liabilities	1,544,000
Total Current Liabilities	**7,753,000**
Long Term Debt	4,203,000
Other Liabilities	4,792,000
Deferred Long Term Liability Charges	646,000
Minority Interest	-
Negative Goodwill	-
Total Liabilities	**17,394,000**
Misc Stocks Options Warrants	-
Redeemable Preferred Stock	-
Preferred Stock	41,000
Common Stock	30,000
Retained Earnings	28,184,000
Treasury Stock	(10,519,000)
Capital Surplus	450,000
Other Stockholder Equity	(952,000)
Total Stockholder Equity	**17,234,000**
Net Tangible Assets	**$10,021,000**

PEPSI
Income Statement

All numbers in thousands

PERIOD ENDING	29-Dec-07
Total Revenue	**39,474,000**
Cost of Revenue	18,038,000
Gross Profit	**21,436,000**
Research Development	-
Selling General and Administrative	14,208,000
Non Recurring	-
Others	58,000
Total Operating Expenses	-
Operating Income or Loss	**7,170,000**
Total Other Income/Expenses Net	685,000
Earnings Before Interest And Taxes	7,855,000
Interest Expense	224,000
Income Before Tax	7,631,000
Income Tax Expense	1,973,000
Minority Interest	-
Net Income From Continuing Ops	5,658,000
Discontinued Operations	-
Extraordinary Items	-
Effect Of Accounting Changes	-
Other Items	-

Net Income	**5,658,000**
Preferred Stock And Other Adjustments	-
Net Income Applicable	
To Common Shares	**$5,658,000**

41030424R00061